HOW TO SATISFY
A WOMAN
<u>EVERY</u> <u>TIME</u>...

and have her beg for more!

HOW TO SATISFY A WOMAN EVERY TIME...

and have her beg for more!

by

NAURA HAYDEN

Bibli O'Phile Publishing Company
New York, New York
Distributed by E. P. Dutton
a division of Penguin, U.S.A.

Published by Bibli O'Phile Publishing Company
P O. Box 5189, New York, New York 10022

Printed in the United States of America

Library of Congress Catalog Card Number: 82-73811

ISBN: 0-942104-01-3

Distributed by E. P. Dutton, a division of Penguin, U.S.A.

To Love, which is God . . .
which is Love . . .
which is God . . .
which is Love . . .
which is God . . .

God, with infinite wisdom, gave us the enchantment
of sex so that together we may joyfully pleasure each
other and create a loving bond that will last a lifetime.

Contents

Contents

HOW TO SATISFY A WOMAN EVERY TIME...

and have her beg for more!

Foreword

I believe in marriage. I also believe in faithfulness in marriage. When one or the other of the partners is unfaithful, the bond of marriage is broken, the trust is shattered. And when that happens, it is difficult if not impossible to keep the marriage alive.

To have a faithful marriage takes two faithful partners. And if *each one* of the partners (not just one) is sexually satisfied, there is no reason to be unfaithful.

I believe God gave us our sex organs to bond us together in pleasure within our marriage. And through this incredible pleasure, to keep us faithful to each other as long as we both shall live.

Almost all women fake orgasms. Women have done this since time began (I give reasons in Chapter 1). Not only are they missing out on one of life's greatest joys, but their husbands and lovers are missing out, too. A woman faking pleasure and a woman pleasured to the depths of her being are two different women. A man's pleasure in sex is magnified tremendously when he has a partner who is giving and receiving the same orgasmic joys, the same explosions of ecstasy, the same expanding of self that carries her to the same far reaches of the universe to which he travels.

A man will be loved as never before when he is able to give his woman the greatest pleasure he can give her—an orgasm. And when he can do this *every time* they make love, her love will know no bounds.

She will never look at another man. She will never need another man. Their union will be bonded as long as they both shall live . . .

Introduction

When I wrote *Isle of View (Say It Out Loud)*, I included in it a short part about sex. After all, the ultimate experience of love is "making love," or sex, between two loving persons. I wrote about THE BIG BANG THEORY, and women faking it. And as I mentioned in the book, I spoke to thousands of women who told me about the problems they had in being satisfied during intercourse by their mates. I interviewed 486 women, not one of whom told me she never faked orgasm. Only 52 told me they occasionally faked it, whereas 124 said they faked it *most* of the time, and 310 said they faked it *every* time. I was astonished, because I thought I was the only one who used to fake it.

I wrote about how a woman can be pleasured so she'll never have to fake it again. I only touched on the subject, I didn't go into real detail. But the response to my TV appearances with the book was overwhelming. I got a letter from a Kansas City newscaster saying that in all his years of broadcasting, he had never had such an incredible response. He said he had hundreds of women and even more *men* calling and writing him asking about that section of my book. And it was the same all over the U.S. TV and radio hosts from Houston, Detroit, Dallas, Minneapolis, Los Angeles, all contacted me with the same phenomenal reactions.

On call-in shows I received hundreds of calls from women, women married eight years, twenty years, thirty-five years, all telling me how they'd been faking it for all the years of their marriages. One woman I'll never forget, who called me on a radio talk show in Miami, told me she'd been married fifty-three years and had never had an orgasm, and had been faking it for all that time. In a darling "little-old-lady-voice" she said very hiply, "You're telling it like it is, Naura!"

A radio host in Cincinnati told me she'd been married fourteen years and had never had an orgasm. Of course, she didn't tell me this on the air; it was during a commercial break (this isn't something you talk about or admit to in public). I spoke to a PR woman in Detroit who was married over twenty years and who had been faking it for over twenty years.

Every male talk-show host who heard these calls was amazed and truly flabbergasted. They all said they couldn't believe it. And the women talk-show hosts told me privately that having orgasm difficulties certainly was true for them, too. In fact, some of them admitted they'd never had one.

Now the reason it's so easy for women to call in and be so brutally frank is because all the calls are anonymous. On call-in radio shows you don't have to give your name, so these women could be ultra-honest about their sex lives.

Women said they were tired of faking it and putting up with THE BIG BANG THEORY, and men said they were anxious to find out how to *really* pleasure their mates so there wouldn't *be* any more faking orgasms.

Isle of View (Say It Out Loud) did very well, and I feel I reached a lot of people. But that section on sex was only a few pages, and I felt that after the incredible responses I had gotten, I needed to expand on what I knew, and bring my experience and help to many more people. I needed to write a book on this very important subject.

There's a need for information that is truly staggering, because this need for satisfying a woman has *never* been explained.

There have been hundreds of books written about how to make love to a *man*. And they all tell about fancy and intricate and sensual things you can do to a man's body to arouse him.

Now the thing that seems a little crazy is that it's really quite *easy* to arouse a man. By nature of his anatomy, arousal is not very difficult. I'm talking about a healthy male—not a physically, mentally, or emotionally sick one. A man's sexual organs are all on the outside of his body and are easily stimulated. Seeing a woman pass by— indeed, *thinking* about seeing a woman pass by—is enough to arouse many men. And looking at a nude female can do more than just make him smile and breathe hard.

Certainly boredom with the same dull partner can turn a man off. At that point he might need technique from a woman to turn him back on. But why is his partner dull? Why is she boring? Can it be that *she* is bored? Out-of-her-skull bored? Because the pleasure is all one-sided? I strongly believe that when a man knows how to please a woman, it becomes a double turn-on, and boredom for both of them flies out the window. Sex only gets boring when one of the partners is not enjoying it.

There have been lots of books written about *sex*, and though they go into foreplay and courting and romance and all that, they *all* miss THE MAIN EVENT. A man can be the greatest romancer and foreplay artist and get his woman aroused, and then comes THE MAIN EVENT and he blunders unknowingly, and the woman, also not knowing what he's doing wrong (but absolutely knowing it's *all* wrong!), pretends finally to have an orgasm because she knows that the way he's doing it she'll *never* have one, and she wants to get the whole thing over with to end the boredom and/or pain.

And there have been lots of books written about how to arouse a woman. They describe foreplay in intimate detail, with all kinds of lotions and props and weird positions and all the things to do to get her ready for an orgasm. But that's only half the story, 'cause as ready as she can get, if the man doesn't know how to handle THE MAIN EVENT—intercourse—she's going to be a *very* frustrated, unhappy, and unsatisfied woman.

And I explain in the first chapter why she will probably fake an orgasm, or else she'll just give up on the relationship. That's when she starts looking around for another man. And can you blame her?

Now I believe *only* a woman can explain the intricacies of satisfying a woman because a man can't *possibly* know this without female input. As I said before, a man, just by nature of his anatomy, is much more easily pleased than a woman. He can't possibly know what the physical sensations are in a woman's body.

And up to now how was a man to learn about

how to pleasure a woman? They sure don't teach it in school. They teach how to read and write and add and subtract and spell. You learn the capitals of every state and where Afghanistan is located, but you sure don't learn how to make love. And as I see it, making love is a lot more important than knowing how to conjugate a verb or parse a sentence. So a man gets out of school and starts dating and probably having sex, and it's all hit-or-miss. He just "does what comes natcherly." He gets satisfaction, but the woman doesn't, because he doesn't know what he's doing. He fumbles and grabs and paws, and because it feels good to him, he thinks it also feels good to her. But it doesn't.

And aside from wishing it felt better, how is the woman to know that it should be any different? She also doesn't learn anything in school about making love. She's just as ignorant as he is.

The vast majority of men are definitely inept lovers, but it's not their fault. You can't blame them. How are they to know any better? And if women were any smarter on the subject, they'd teach the men. But they aren't, so the men keep groping and the women keep faking.

Another major reason for the gross ignorance about sex is that almost all romantic novels dealing with scenes of explicit sex are written by men who believe that women love rough, tough, bang-'em-up sex, or by women who, having read these kinds of stories, also think that's what will turn on their readers. After all, it does *sound* sexy.

Why is it that everyone thinks a woman just needs a man to *enter* her to make her roll around wild-eyed in a crazed fashion and scream out in passion? I've read it hundreds of times, and that's the main reason I thought there was something wrong with *me* when I didn't have an orgasm after being "banged." I was brainwashed by writers of sexy fiction, and that's *just* what it is—fiction. *Playboy* and *Penthouse* and all the other men's magazines lead everyone to think that every really sensuous woman needs only to have a man enter her to have her scream with passion and writhe with desire.

Some of the following excerpts are fiction, and some purport to be true. I listed a lot of them because there are so many in every book and magazine around. And as many as I listed, I left out literally thousands more. Some are very well written and some are awful. But they *all* make my point.

"She arched both legs girdling his hips, and impaled herself on him . . . he bore down, her nails knifing his skin, until he pierced her . . . she began to thrust at Fabian, her body springing back as the tip of his flesh met her womb . . . her body sundered, waiting for him to keel into her, offering herself to a deeper quest . . . As she plunged beneath him, her eyes staring, her mouth trapping a scream, he moved into her again, a reeling of ebb and flow pulling her apart, buckling her in quivers of desire . . ."

Passion Play Jerzy Kosinski

"He pushed her legs apart with his hands, and she lay before him, spread-eagled. He mounted her. 'I'm going to plug you, you bitch.' His cock was enormous . . . Then there was only ecstasy . . . as she watched his waxen cock moving in and out . . . 'Don't take it away,' she screamed. 'I love it. Keep fucking me . . . I love it, I love it . . . I love your gigantic, beautiful prick, your hairy cock. I want it to plug me forever.' "

The Users Joyce Haber

"As I entered her ass, she gave a soft moan of pleasure and begged me to go deeper. 'Ram it up me. Please, ram it harder! Harder! Harder!' Soon my thrusts were so forceful that each one nearly knocked her over . . . As we reached orgasm, we were both moaning so loudly that we nearly drowned out the music . . ."

Name and Address Withheld
Penthouse Forum, May 1980

"She was so hot by the time they had gotten to her cabin that as he untied her bikini the very touch of his hand on her flesh caused her to shudder with orgasm."

The Body Brokers Robert Eaton

"I positioned myself over her and started to thrust gently, but Linda would have none of that. She grabbed me by my ass and pulled me toward her so that my full seven inches were firmly embedded in her cunt. I started to thrust in and out . . . until Linda started to lift her ass off the floor to meet my thrusts. She had to be the best fuck of my life, because she really got into it, not like most of the women I've fucked, who seem to be very passive and require a lot of foreplay."

B.G., Chicago, Illinois
Penthouse Forum, May 1980

"His lovemaking became frenetic, almost savage, but Karen, later, exhausted and sleepy, told him he was terrific . . ."

Count Me In Fan Nichols

"She lurched her bottom up and locked her legs around his back. He lowered himself into her and she began to writhe and grind her pelvis up against him, muttering strange guttural sounds and grunts of pleasure . . . In a few moments they were thrusting and churning their bodies in a frenzy of excitement . . . then she pushed herself down until she caught up his rigid member again and plunged herself upon it, bouncing up and down, flexing her legs, now squatting, now kneeling. Suddenly she attained a shuddering climax."

Runaway Slave Robert Tralins

"Kevin . . . abruptly flipped me onto my back, entering me with one hard thrust. As he began pumping furiously . . . I wrapped my legs around him and I could feel myself climbing to the heights of ecstasy . . . In two more fierce thrusts he joined me in the climax of a truly beautiful fuck."

L.L., Jacksonville, Florida
Penthouse Forum, May 1980

". . . He pulled his hand away, and without a pause at all, literally rammed his cock in her cunt so hard it caused his balls to strike her tummy, and a low animal growl of pleasure emanated from her pelvis and erupted . . ."

"Troy," *Men In Love* Nancy Friday

"I barely got the head of my ten-inch member into her when she pleaded with me to stop, but of course I did not. I fucked her ass so hard that I thought she would never walk again, but somehow she handled it and begged me for more."

Name and Address Withheld
Penthouse Forum, May 1980

"With no warning, no gentle probe, he shoved his prick into Jana and fell on her simultaneously . . . He lifted himself out of her slightly and then fell again more deeply into her . . . grinding his hips into hers . . . pushing in and out, his balls slapping at the skin between her thighs. Jana smiled."

Trading Up Joan Lea

"By this time she was begging for someone to ram a cock in her. I obliged and rammed all eight inches in and gave her a ride."

Name and Address Withheld
Penthouse Forum, May 1980

"Jack gripped her and drove himself into her. She clutched at him, trying not to scream, and she felt how wildly, helplessly they struggled, how viciously her body grabbed at his in its agony to keep him with her, to force him with her, to force him again and again into her. How she needed him, how raw and crazy was her need for him."

Do With Me What You Will
Joyce Carol Oates

"He fucked like a machine, refusing to succumb to an orgasm himself but urging me to come again and again and again. After the first three times I was sore and wanted to stop. I begged him to stop but he wouldn't.

He kept banging away at me like an ax murderer."

Fear of Flying Erica Jong

"Hildy begged me to fuck her. I thrust my huge nine and one-half inch tool into her viselike box. We fucked with a vengeance for what seemed hours. She experienced dozens of orgasms."

T.R.H., Washington, D.C.
Penthouse Forum, May 1980

"She started bouncing on him, a crazy rhythm, leading him on, and on, bouncing and feinting like the tough, punch-crazy fighter she was, till she got him locked in her hug again, poised for her shuddering come."

Doctor Love Gael Greene

"I inserted my swollen member into her love triangle and started to pump her. We climaxed at the same time . . ."

Name and Address Withheld
Penthouse Forum, May 1980

"Beau began fucking her hard and then built up momentum. 'No, no, yes, yes,' she muttered. Dear God, this awful pleasure was driving her mad. Joy and pain were intertwined. 'Oh, oh, no, Mr. Kingston, I'm coming—oh—oh.' Miss Holmes' thin body was writhed in ecstasy."

March to the Drummer Peter Dane

Because none of the above quotes is the way it really happens, I'm going to start right out in Chapters 1, 2, and 3 in my book with *explicit instructions* on how a woman can be *really* satisfied. I *guarantee* that if you read them carefully and go about making love as I suggest, you will absolutely, positively be successful in pleasuring your woman *every time*.

And it will be quicker, too. Most men don't have a clue to what they're doing to a woman's body in the sex department, and because of this ineptness, they think it has to take hours to satisfy her. The beauty part of all this is that when a man finds out *exactly* what to do—and does it—it takes just minutes for a woman to

have an orgasm once THE MAIN EVENT begins.

And it works. It really does!

How can I guarantee positive results every
time? You just read on, put into practice what
I've explained, and you'll find out the very first
time that it absolutely does work. *Every time!*

1
The Big Bang Theory

Okay, you two are in love, and you're making love. It's fabulous for you—the guy—it's sensual, pleasure-full, and your orgasm is incredible. You love her and you know she also loves you and she says it's great for her, too.

But is it? I'm sure you believe her, and feel that you could tell if she were faking, but you probably don't know that there's *no way* a man can tell if a woman is faking an orgasm. I'm sure you've heard that there *are* ways to tell, like her breathing quickening, her nipples getting hard, etc., but all these things happen when she's aroused, not necessarily when she has an orgasm.

And all you women. You know you can fake it, right? You've been doing it for years. God knows I was. Up till several years ago, I had *never* had an orgasm in the normal way of making love. (The other ways are not abnormal. I use the term normal to mean the usual, or most common way, of making love, the missionary position. I believe that *this* is the most sexually satisfying to both men and women once the man learns how to really pleasure his mate in this position. Certainly all other ways are pleasure-full, but they gained their great popularity because it is easier for a woman to be satisfied using *some* sort of manipulation of her clitoris, either manually— with fingers—or with lips and a tongue. And women have gotten their men to do these things because they know from experience that's the *only* way they can achieve orgasm. Even though it *is* pleasure-full, it doesn't *begin* to feel as totally and completely satisfying as the normal missionary position, once the man learns how to make love in this wonderful and loving way.)

Again, I had *never* had an orgasm in the normal way of making love. And I faked it. I had faked it all my life. Believe me, I was Bernhardt, Duse, Bette Davis, Faye Dunaway, and Sissy Spacek all rolled up in one. No man ever suspected, *ever,* that I wasn't thoroughly, totally satisfied. And that's because I was such a great actress convincing him. I moaned, I writhed, I gritted my teeth, I did *all* the right things at the right times—and I was completely and utterly unsatisfied and frustrated.

Now some of you men might ask why—why did I go to all that trouble? Why didn't I just tell my guy that I wasn't being satisfied? I didn't for the same reasons that *no* woman wants to tell her guy.

First, she loves her man—really cares for him—and that's why they're together in the first place. And she doesn't want to hurt his feelings or his ego. She wants him to feel like a tiger.

Second, she doesn't want him to feel she's not a sensual woman, that maybe there's something wrong with her. She thinks it's her fault, that maybe she's a "frigid" woman. Why else is she unable to have an orgasm when he has such an easy time having one? God forbid the thought should ever cross *his* mind that she's "frigid." That would devastate her. (At this point I'd like to point out that there is *no* such thing as a "frigid" woman. There are only inept male lovers!) And in her mind, if he *did* think she was "frigid," he might go out looking for a hot number to replace her.

And third, she doesn't know *why* she's not having an orgasm. She still thinks it's her fault, but if she only knew *why,* she could do something about it, right? Or she could tell *him* what to do right if she only knew what he was doing wrong, or that he *was* doing something wrong. He got her excited with foreplay. She's burning up with desire, and as soon as he enters her and starts pumping, she's turned off. That wonderful, excited feeling, that glow all over her body, that tingling in her sex organs, vanishes. Why? Because he's doing his BIG BANG number. In and out, in and out—Bang Bang. He doesn't realize it doesn't feel good to her. It doesn't always hurt at first, but it sure doesn't feel terrific. And after a while of being "banged," it *does* hurt, and she wishes he would get it over with fast!

If you men would just try this experiment, you'd understand exactly what it feels like. Put your left arm out and with your right fist hit your left arm for about thirty seconds (the longer you do it, the more it hurts). I did this on several TV shows to show the male hosts what "banging" feels like, and they were all amazed. They had no idea that that's what happens when a man enters a woman and starts pumping. But if you stop and think about it, it's very logical. A man's penis, ready to make love, is hard. The territory surrounding his penis, his pelvis, is also hard. And a woman's sex organs are all soft. So when a man puts his hard organ into a woman's soft organ and then starts pumping hard, it hits her hard on her clit, and it doesn't feel good. After a few minutes of being hit on her soft organ, it begins to hurt. And just to get it over with, she'll pretend *anything* to stop the pain or boredom. She quickly learns how to pretend she's having an orgasm.

In the next two chapters I'm going to tell you *exactly* what to do to not only arouse your woman, but to take her all the way to the most glorious orgasm she's ever had, and to do this *every time you make love.*

And the beauty part of this is that when she truly has an incredible orgasm that sends off rockets through her whole body, *you* will become more excited than you've ever been before, and your orgasm will surpass any you've ever had before, because now you'll know the real power that you possess to turn her on and send her to the moon, outer space, Mars, Venus, etc. And you'll feel a love from her that you've never felt before.

And even if you think you're pretty good now, and your woman tells you that you're a perfect lover, (remember, she loves you and wants you to think you *are* perfect), try it anyway!

And if you've been worried that maybe she's got eyes for someone else, or think maybe she *might* look at another man, after you give her the ultimate pleasure that you're now capable of because *now* you know *how* to pleasure her, you'll realize that there's no *reason* for her to look around or to fool around, 'cause *you're* the man who gives her what she wants and needs and loves.

2
Teasing

Stop and think about what turns you on. A sniff of a wonderful fragrance, a taste of caviar, the touch of velvet on your skin—all soft and gentle things. It's not so pleasure-full to be overpowered by too strong an odor (yech!), or to gorge on a full can of caviar (double yech!!!), or to be rubbed roughly with any material—velvet included.

Try another experiment. Put your left arm out again and now take the fingers of your right hand and very softly run your fingers over your arm. But *very* gently. Hardly touch the skin. Make like your fingers are feathers, and tease your skin. It tickles a little, and after a few seconds you feel like you want to scratch it. The soft touch makes a gentle itch which feels good, and needs to be satisfied, or scratched.

Well, the same principle applies to making love. First, gently touch her skin—anywhere. A leg, an arm, her back—anywhere. But it *must* be gentle, very soft and teasy. Spend a minute or two there. Then slowly, *very* slowly, work up to her breasts—softly, with the tips and pads of your fingers. But don't touch her nipples—yet!

Create a desire. Make her sweetly suffer with wanting something so badly and not being able to get it when she wants it. Make her sweetly suffer with a desire that you won't give her . . . yet.

When you paw her or roughly maul her (which I call THREEPLAY—cause it sure ain't fore-play!), that's a turn-off, like too strong an odor. *Deliberately* don't touch her nipples for a few minutes. Deliberately tease her. And after a few minutes of your teasing her—above her nipple, below it, and all around it, but *never* right on it, she'll be ready for you to touch it. But *only* softly touch, don't grab or pull or knead. Again, just softly take your fingers and hardly touch at all. This will begin to drive her crazy. You are teasing her. Keep it up, knowing you're driving her crazy. You are calling the shots and that alone is a giant turn-on. And the soft tease of your fingers makes her want more. The fact that you're holding back, and only gently teasing with the soft touch of your fingers, creates a *divine itch*, an unbelievably strong itch, and the more it itches, the more she wants you to satisfy that itch. By holding back, you are creating a tremendous desire within all of her sex organs. After a few minutes of this (and *don't* weaken, and grab or paw), whenever you feel she's ready (and believe me, she'll let you know), if *you're* ready with an aroused and hard penis (if not, I'll cover that a little later—right now we're working on *her*)—if you're ready with an aroused and hard penis, *do not put it in her!* This is THE MAIN EVENT coming up, and once you get this right, you'll never have trouble again.

3
The Main Event

Now you are aroused. Your penis is aroused. And she is aroused.

DO NOT ENTER HER.

Take your penis in your hand and gently rub her clitoris with it. Gently. *Very* gently. Play with her with your penis very softly. You are letting her know that you *could* go inside her with it, but you're choosing not to. You are going to tease her with it. You are going to build a desire inside her until she begs you to put it in. You are now totally in charge—the master of your self and of her. You are going to tease her until she literally will beg you to put it in.

You'll be getting to that point soon. You're teasing her clit gently and the more you tease, the more aroused she's getting. Just keep it up, *very* gently teasing her with your penis. She's now asking you to put it in, and you say no, and you keep teasing her with your penis gently rubbing on her clit. Again she asks you to put it in, and again you say no. You continue teasing her and now she says *please* put it in, but you're *still* not ready. You want her to beg, right? Well, give her another minute or so and she will beg. Now remember, you're in charge. It's *your* penis and you can sweetly torture her as long as you want.

And she'll *love* it. She knows you're in charge and in total control of your penis and her body. Before this you were *not* in control. You just shoved it in—Bang Bang—and that was it. No control. No mastery.

All right, now you've finally gotten her to the point of begging you to put it in. So you've decided the time is now. But do you put it in?

NO!

You will *very* gently go in about one-half inch (hardly at all) and then slowly take it out, then slowly back in one-half inch and slowly out again. She's going to be really going crazy by now—

and you're going to love it. And so will she. After all, she never felt like *this* before.

Good grief, does she want you! But you're still in charge and still teasing.

Now you'll put it in one inch and slowly out, and in one inch and slowly out. Now go in a little more, *very* slowly. Maybe one and a half inches. And very slowly out. Don't *ever* go in all the way, till she starts having her orgasm. Just keep teasing her. When you've worked up to *almost* the full length of your penis, slowly withdraw and in again and out again—*very* slowly and very gently.

> The reason not to go all the way in with your penis is that when you do, it rams against her clit, and the whole purpose of this is to *tease* her clit—not to hit it, but to create a desire that drives her mad until she has an orgasm.

Now you're still slowly going in and out, *never* all the way, and you can feel her getting more and more aroused. This in turn gets you more and more aroused, because as much as you're teasing her, you're teasing your self, too. You're totally in command, and both of you know it. And the more you can stall it, the more incredible and intense will be both your orgasms.

Teasing is a form of sweet torture, for both of you. And we all—both men and women—have a touch of masochism within us. The act of surrender, which is the most beautiful part of orgasm, is surrender in love to the one you love.

> Now if you want to try something that is sexually incredible, but incredibly difficult to do, get to the point you're at now—the point where you're both seconds away from an orgasm, and stop. Just stop cold. And resume several hours later, or the next morning. Holding back like that will triply excite you when you resume your lovemaking, and you'll both be so sensual and so ready that when you start over again with the teasing, you'll both be tortured with desire, and by the time you gently tease her clit with your penis, she'll be screaming for you to enter her, and when you start gently putting your penis

in her a half-inch at a time, she'll be pleading, begging for you to go in more. And when you both have your orgasms, the explosions will rock both of you like you've never been rocked before.

But it takes great control. And a very healthy body (see Chapter 7).

Okay, you've brought her to the point of surrender—she's begging you to give her the orgasm that her body so desperately wants now, so now you go in just a little deeper, and slowly out, and keep that up until her body begins to quiver, and you will continue going in and out while she has an orgasm that rocks her whole being. She may moan or scream on talk incoherently or just breathe huskily, but this time you'll know she's not faking it. You have *made* her have an orgasm. It wasn't an accident. It didn't just happen. You deliberately and consciously teased her body until she couldn't stand it any longer. She gave her self to you totally and completely because you demanded it. With love, to be sure, but it was a deliberate command for her to respond. She opened up completely to you.

Now if you're in good physical shape, you'll be able to give her several more orgasms after her first one. The ones that follow come much faster and you don't have to tease. Of course, you can't revert to THE BIG BANG, but you can be a *little* more forceful. You'll see how she'll react if you can keep from coming and continue to penetrate her. Usually, within a minute she'll have another and another, as long as you can continue. Usually three to five—some women only two and some over five.

But maybe you're so excited by her first explosion that you just can't hold back, so you have your orgasm. It will be the deepest and fullest orgasm you've ever had, because you've controlled it up to this moment, and you've teased your self and now you've let your self go.

Hopefully, you've been able to give her two or three orgasms, but if only one, that's okay, 'cause it was undoubtedly the best one she's ever had, maybe even her first. And next time you can try for more than one.

You'll notice how relaxed she is and how loving toward you. After all, you've just given her the greatest experience of her life. And she'll never forget it. Or you.

4
What To Do If Your Man Won't Even Try

(For Women Only!)

If you're a woman and can't get your mate to read this book (he doesn't read books, he doesn't read sex books, he already knows how to make love, he knows some women fake it but *you* sure don't, etc.), *you* read it, and after *you* learn what he's been doing wrong all these years, you'll now be able to gently and sneakily show him what you want, or if you're in love with a *real* hardhead who refuses to change *anything* about the way he makes love, and he's so stubborn he's hanging on to his "great lover" image, all is not lost.

49

You should *not* continue faking it. In fact, if you do, you'll be letting your man down, because then he'll *never* learn how inept he is, and he'll *never* change, and *you'll* never have the ecstasy of an orgasm during intercourse. You'll also be letting your *self* down by pretending something that isn't happening.

In Shere Hite's book *The Hite Report,* she lists hundreds of quotes from women who fake it. Here are just a few that might ring a bell:

"I fake orgasms to save his pride and prevent arguments."

"Sometimes it builds a man's ego to let him think he's successful. Therefore, if I really like a man and want him to think I enjoyed sex more than I did, I do it."

"Yes, I always fake orgasms. It just seems polite. Why be rude?"

"I fake them often. He and I have had such an abysmal sex relationship that I don't want to burden him with the knowledge that I don't come during intercourse."

"I *always* did. (I'm sixty-two now.) I was told to do it by male doctors to keep my husband happy (bless me). I was thinking there was something missing in my makeup for about thirty-five years—and that's a long time to imagine you had to fake it!"

"I have been faking orgasms for thirty years, because I need approval—I lack self-esteem—I'm ashamed as though I had a club foot or one eye—and because I don't want to hurt my husband, who is also insecure."

"I always fake them during intercourse. I know it would hurt the guy I live with if he knew otherwise, so I always tell him that it was great."

"Yes, it's easier and faster than struggling."

"When he asked if I came, I said yes. Sometimes he would even tell me how many times I came, and I didn't have the heart to tell him that I hadn't come at all."

51

"I always fake them—because I never have them."

"Like asking if the sky is blue. Yes, during intercourse; I usually don't want men to know I *never* have them."

"For fifteen years I was the world's best faker. Honestly—I think they should have a phallic trophy—mounted on a pedestal (like in the art history books) for *all women*—I think they all fake it with men."

As I mentioned earlier in the book, up till a few years ago, I had never had an orgasm during intercourse and I *always* faked it. And I honestly thought I was the only woman doing this. Of course, I never ever told a single soul, man or woman, that I was not able to orgasm in intercourse. I was embarrassed and I didn't want *anyone* to know that I was not "normal"—HA! This was a little before everyone talked so freely about sex, and before all the very explicit books were written about women's sexual problems. So from all I read in popular fiction and from all I heard, I certainly thought all other women had an easy time climaxing during intercourse. All my friends and acquaintances must have been as anxiety-ridden as I was about this lack in their lives, and they sure weren't going to tell me or anyone else about their "frigidity problem." They obviously were as upset and embarrassed as I was, and they were all faking it exactly the same as I was.

The difference now is that because women are admitting their problems, probably very few think they are the only ones faking it. Hopefully, even fewer think they're "frigid."

Here are some more quotes from *The Hite Report* about how so many women think they are, or thought they were, "frigid":

"I went along for thirty-four years carrying the burden of not having vaginal orgasms, never telling anyone because I felt something was wrong with me—I thought I was frigid."

". . . It's going to take some time, and I believe eventually a woman will have to tell me how to have an orgasm during sex. Right now I don't know who to ask plus I will have to be quite careful in discussing this—because I wouldn't want someone to think I was abnormal."

"I fake them to avoid confrontation with a man, to avoid explaining why I was like I was, to avoid their trite responses of lesbianism, frigidity, etc."

"Yes, for ten and a half years! I didn't want anyone to think I was frigid."

". . . if I don't have any—then it's my fault, and my boyfriend doesn't want to have intercourse very much if I am frigid."

In *The Redbook Report on Female Sexuality,* a woman is quoted about her unhappy and unsatisfied sex life, and what her doctor told her about it:

". . . After 10 years of never having an orgasm, I finally got up the courage to ask my family doctor (they always tell you to ask the family doctor, right?), as my marriage was falling apart. His response was, 'Seventy percent of all women are frigid—it's all in your head.' "

Just as I thought it was only *my* problem (never dreaming it could *possibly* be my man's ineptness), these women all think they are, or thought they were, "frigid."

Again, please remember, *there is no such thing as a frigid woman*. Once men really learn how to intercourse, *every woman will respond!*

Now lots of women think they have to masturbate during intercourse to achieve orgasm, but this is *not* true. When you get your man to make love exactly as in Chapter 3, you do not have to do *anything* to your self—he does it all. Here are just a few quotes from *The Hite Report* about women who orgasm during intercourse, but *only* with masturbation.

"I would like to have orgasm during intercourse *without* having to play with my clitoris at the same time! If I didn't do that I would almost never come."

". . . I have orgasms from masturbation and clitoral stimulation *only*. I feel very little, and rarely, from penis penetration, and I've *never* had an orgasm from penis stimulation . . ."

"I would like to have orgasm during intercourse *without* having to play with my clitoris at the same time. If I didn't do that I would almost never have orgasms. I would like to be able to have them with just intercourse . . ."

In *The Redbook Report on Female Sexuality*, the authors state:

"Should intercourse be taken literally—orgasms that occur during penetration—or generally—orgasms that occur during a sexual episode, including manual or oral stimulation? The distinction is not trivial for the millions of women who are easily orgasmic by mouth, hand, and vibrator but for whom the penis is just a pleasant accompaniment to the blissful harmonies."

"I have conducted my own little survey and I do not have one friend or acquaintance who has ever had a "real" orgasm through intercourse—only through clitoral stimulation . . ."

"I have never had an orgasm during sexual intercourse. To have an orgasm, I must have cunnilingus or manual clitoral stimulation. I know of women today who are faking orgasm during intercourse because they are too embarrassed to tell their husbands or lovers that no matter how long they keep their erection, they just can't make her have an orgasm. *Please, please* discuss this when you print the results of your survey! . . ."

Dr. Seymour Fisher, who wrote *The Female Orgasm,* did a study of over three hundred women, and of these women, 80 percent said they needed masturbation during intercourse in order to have an orgasm.

Alfred Kinsey of the "Kinsey Report"—*(Sexual Behavior in the Human Female)* reported that "the techniques of masturbation and of petting are more specifically calculated to effect orgasm than the techniques of coitus itself." Kinsey says that for most women, intercourse alone always or almost always results in *no* orgasm, and that intercourse with masturbation for these same women almost always results in orgasm.

Dr. Debora Phillips, who wrote *Sexual Confidence*, says:

> ". . . a woman is less likely to have an orgasm during intercourse than through manual or oral stimulation. (For those who would rush into intercourse as the *goal* of lovemaking, it's interesting to note that many women actually experience a *decline* in sexual pleasure with penetration.)"

Dr. Helen Singer Kaplan, Dr. David Reuben, Masters and Johnson, have all written about masturbation as a means of attaining orgasm during intercourse for most women who cannot climax without it.

So—your mate is a lousy lover who won't admit it or change, you found out you *don't* have to masturbate during intercourse, and you're *not* going to fake it anymore. What *are* you going to do?

You are now going to take charge of the situation, and by doing this, control your love life and be sexually satisfied every time you make love.

Of course, solving your own problem by your self is *not* as sensational as having a loving partner who tries to change and become a better lover because he accepts and admits the fact that he's inept. Listen, almost every man is, so it's nothing to be ashamed about. He never wanted to be, and till now he didn't really realize that he was inept. But hopefully he's read this book and is willing to try to make you happy.

But your problem now is that you are in love with a *real BIG BANG* artist, and he can't (or won't) accept the fact that he's a terrible lover. And you're so much in love with him that you want to stick with him, awful lover or not. So what do you do?

Well, first of all, you *don't* tell him he's inept. In fact, no woman should *ever* tell her man that he's been a bad lover. Even if you've been faking it for thirty-five years, don't ever tell him that. Why hurt him now? After all, he wasn't inept deliberately, and you didn't know what to tell him to do either, right? The point is you can't do anything about the past—it's all over with and you can't recapture all those missed ecstasies— so let's start with *NOW*. Again, hopefully he's read this book and is now a fantastic lover (it's so *easy* to be one once you know what to do and what not to do).

So *now* for how a woman can control her sexual destiny, can have a climax every time with a man who hasn't picked up on, or refuses to learn, teasing.

You do it with your thighs. When a man comes on too strong and too hard and starts banging, just squeeze your thighs, which will clamp around his hips and keep his body from ramming your body, and slow him down. Slowly, as he finds out he can't "bang" you because you won't *allow* it, he'll start to ease up his attack because he really can't do anything else.

Now when I say squeeze your thighs, I mean *take control.* You have some very strong thigh muscles there that are hardly ever used, and the more you use them, the stronger they get. When you squeeze your thighs, you also control how much of his penis you allow inside you. Not only will he not be able to ram you, he will only be able to go in as much and as far as you want. So you can tease your self with his penis and do all the things that in Chapter 3 *he* will do to you, only now *you're* in charge. It's not as super-duper as when *he* does it all, but you definitely can have an orgasm this way, and he will undoubtedly eventually become aware of what you want and what pleasures you.

Once you have shown a man that you know what you want, and he starts to pick up on it, and he knows that you know what you want, and he begins, gently and lovingly, to move in and out, you can begin to relax and let him take over more. And every time you make love and show him what you want and how you want it, he will subconsciously begin to remember, so that each time he'll bang a little less hard and you won't have to flex those thigh muscles as hard. Eventually (hopefully after only the first time, but maybe it'll take two or three times), he will totally understand how you *don't* want him to bang you, and how you *do* want him to make love to you in a really teasy and loving way. When a woman is physically relaxed, she will be mentally and emotionally relaxed, too. If he gets too rough again, just flex those thigh muscles to signal him to gentle it (not that maybe later you won't want it a little stronger, but you *start* with it teasy). Then, as he gently and lovingly and teasingly makes love, you can relax and begin to surrender your self to him, slowly, as he will to you. Sexual surrender is the ultimate in trust— and the ultimate in pleasure. When you're totally open physically, trusting mentally, and vulnerable emotionally is when the rockets explode.

And exploding rockets with the one you love is what life is all about!

5
Lovingness

I'm a total romantic. I believe in everything romantic. I believe love is the most important thing in the world. I know it is for me.

Whenever I talk about sex, I mean sex with love. Without love, sex is an exercise—a pleasant one, to be sure—but still just an exercise.

Aah, but sex with love . . . that's the greatest experience in the world—bar none! I can't think of one thing that feels better physically, mentally, or emotionally.

Now the ability to love is something we all have, but not all of us use it. There are lots of reasons for this. We're afraid, we're tense, we're angry, we're anxious, we're depressed.

Unfortunately, all of these negatives keep us from being loving. So it's up to all of us to try as hard as we can to get rid of all the negs in our lives. In Chapter 7 I cover the physical part of health, and I believe when the body is *truly* healthy, then the mind and emotions will be healthy, too.

So in this chapter I don't want to talk about feeling *loving*, but feeling *loved*. Receptive to love. Opening your self to love. Not feeling guilty or unworthy of love.

I believe strongly in God (or Good, or Giant Self, or Spirit, or anything you want to call Him/ Her/It); in fact, my belief in God is the strongest belief in my life, the one thing I'm positive of. And I strongly believe that God gives us everything in life we need, at the moment we need it. We may need to learn something, so God gives us a tool with which to learn our lesson. The tool may be pain, or loss of a job, or loss of a loved one, or anything which may *appear* to be negative, but is in reality only a tool that God sends us so that we can use that tool and learn.

I don't believe in guilt. I don't think *any* negative is a part of God. And guilt is a negative. We're not supposed to feel sorry we did something. After all, if we *could* have done something different at the time, we *would* have. But we didn't, we did what we had to do at that moment. We're supposed to learn from what we did. We're not supposed to feel unworthy of *anything*, which is what guilt makes us feel.

God created us perfect—we're the ones who screw up. And the only reason we screw up is because we don't fully realize that we are God's children. If we really and truly believe and feel that God loves us and protects us and guides us, how could we *ever* feel afraid, or lost, or angry, or guilty, or depressed, or *any* of the negative feelings? So the whole point is to work on a *real* positive—the ultimate positive—the knowledge and feeling and assurance that we are part of God and God is in all of us, and that God adores each one of us and wants us to feel only positive things in our lives. And the more we can work at feeling the closeness to God, the sooner we can feel and think and have these things.

I don't believe that God just loves me—I

believe that God *adores* me and wants me to
have everything I want. And I do an emotional
exercise every day of my life that brings me
closer and closer to God every day of my life. I
wrote a little about this in *Isle of View (Say It Out
Loud)*, but it's so important to me that I'd like to
repeat it. I feel so strongly about this exercise,
and I know how tremendously it's helped me to
achieve the things I want, that I want to convince
you to try it. It only takes several minutes a day,
but it colors your whole day in such a positive
light that once you begin doing it, I think you'll do
it the rest of your life. You, too, will begin to feel
differently, and you'll begin to think differently.
You'll also begin to get a lot of things that you've
wanted for a long time.

It's actually a form of self-hypnosis, and when
you start to use your conscious mind in this
exercise, you will be feeding input into your
subconscious mind. You will start to relax when
you let God run your life, trusting that everything you want and need will be given to you
when you need it. You'll stop pushing so hard out
of fear, because once you feel, actually *feel*, that

God loves you, you can't experience fear. You can't feel love and fear at the same time.

Here is my emotional exercise that I do *every* day of my life.

Every morning, at the end of my twenty sit-ups on my slant-board, I just lie there and close my eyes and totally relax (if you don't have a slant-board, you can lie flat on your bed, without a pillow.) Then I remember emotionally what it was like when someone *really* loved me (mother, father, husband, wife—it makes no difference who, but you must remember the *feeling* of being loved, the wonderful physical glow, and warmth, and open feeling, of someone truly loving you). This takes real concentration and you must be relaxed, but it's really fun. Just be still and go back in time and remember incidents of being held by your mother, or hugged by your dad, or praised by either one of them. You might remember lying on a beach as a kid, under a warm sky, and seeing your mother or dad, and feeling secure and warm and loved with them sitting nearby. It doesn't matter *how* you recapture the feeling of being loved, as long as *something* in your past warms you and opens you up emotionally in its memory.

When I've captured this warm feeling, I smile, and say, "God adores me," and then I smile bigger and keep that *great* feeling of openness and warmth. You don't have to *try* to smile—when you feel *really* loved, you can't *help* but smile. Then I say, "God adores me and wants me to have *everything* I want." Now, follow my logic—assuming that God, or Love, or Giant Self, exists, and *really* loves me (which we've been taught mentally but not emotionally), He/She/It certainly wants me to have everything I want and need. My darling mother wants me to have everything she can give me; when my father was alive, he loved me dearly and wanted me to have anything and everything my little heart desired. So God, who *adores* me (I like the word "adore" better than "love" in this case, because it seems stronger to me to emotionally capture the feeling—but you can use love or cherish or *any* word that works for you), so God who adores me wants me to have everything in the whole world that I want.

Now I get into a little more detail. "God adores me and wants me to have everything I want"—then I list all the things I want (and you pick all the things you've ever really wanted, and realize that if God *does* adore you, you'll get all these terrific things—success, love, a joyful marriage, friends, money, a great job, a terrific apartment, gorgeous clothes, fame, an emerald bracelet, a new car, a baby). Whoever *really* loved you would have given you *anything* you wanted, right? And if God *adores* you, and you not only believe it but you *feel* it, that feeling will grow till you feel more and more loved, and you feel more and more deserving of everything you want. It's very important to smile broadly, because that'll help you to feel loved and happy. Again, you don't force a smile—when you feel truly loved, you can't *help* but smile! So when you're relaxed and smiling, you'll know the right feeling is there.

My biggest problem was that I never felt I deserved anything. I felt only guilt for wanting good things for my self. Maybe it was my super-religious upbringing with hell and guilt, etc., or maybe it came from somewhere else, but there it was, coloring everything I did. No wonder I repelled my self from getting good things from my life—I didn't feel I deserved them. But doing this emotional exercise *every day*, and without exception, makes me know I'm loved, and makes me *feel* like I'm a lovable person who deserves everything I want.

And every single day I feel more and more loved, and more and more lovable, and this *automatically* makes me a more loving person.

Feeling loved makes you realize the *goodness* within your self, and that goodness is your REAL SELF, or my GIANT SELF, as I call God.

Feeling loved makes you feel your oneness with God.

6
Fantasies

Fantasies are wonderful. They take ordinary experiences and transform them into imaginative flights to the unknown. They can be exciting, sexy, erotic, stimulating, fun, relaxing—all kinds of different things.

We all fantasize about a new car, a gorgeous mansion, a yacht of our own to take us to our own private tropical island where we'll never have to work again. Just get up, pick breakfast, swim in the lagoon, laze in the sun, make love, and sleep a peaceful sleep under the stars.

Where our fantasies start differing in sex is how we see ourselves. Some men fantasize about power in love, and some women fantasize about helplessness in love. However, I've known men who fantasize about helplessness and are very passive in sex, and I've known women who fantasize about power and are very active in sex. And I'm not talking about very weak men and very strong women. Some of the strongest, most successful men in business, real titans of industry, want to be treated as pussy-cats and fantasize all kinds of masochistic de-lights (to them), and some of the weakest-appearing, most docile types of women are tigers and fantasize power. So you can't tell from looks or appearances.

A fantasy is just that—imaginative. It can't hurt you or anyone else, because it's all in your mind.

Now I don't think fantasizing someone else in place of the person you're with is constructive. That's negative, not positive. After all, if you'd rather be with someone else, you shouldn't be with the person you're with.

And of course I believe totally in faithfulness, so that precludes fantasizing group sex.

Really constructive fantasizing is taking the

person you're actually with and imagining a situation with him or her that turns you on—really stimulates you mentally, emotionally, and sexually.

How can that be bad? You're using your power of imagination (mind's dominant power) and using it to put excitement into a *real* situation. And if you feel like telling your partner what turns you on, go ahead and do it. If not, don't.

Some women fantasize being spanked. If you've always wanted to imagine this and it seems your partner is just not the type, well, use your vivid imagination (*all* imaginations are vivid, and like a muscle, they get stronger with use, so the more you use your imagination, the more vivid it becomes). Fantasize your man as the type who *would* want to spank you. And realize that every person, man or woman, reacts differently in different situations. What may appear as a Casper Milquetoast or Wilbur Wimp may have all kinds of strong and kinky desires lurking beneath the surface. Just use your imagination and realize that it *is* possible—he *could* be harboring a secret desire to spank you. You don't have to tell him what you want (unless you decide you'd like to). You can just keep fantasizing all you want and he'll never know what's going on inside your mind.

And then again, you may not know what's going on in *his* brain either. He may have an incredible imagination and may be fantasizing you doing all kinds of wonderful things to him.

For instance, lots of men love to imagine that their woman is stronger than they are, and capable of ordering the man to do the woman's bidding—*whatever* it is. Some *men* like to fantasize being spanked by their wives. It really turns them on.

Now lots of women also fantasize having tremendous power to order their men to do whatever they want. Some women use their own sense of power as an aphrodisiac (power *can* be a turn-on!). They *like* imagining that they are more powerful than their husbands and can force little husbies to do their bidding. Now remember, this is all fantasy—we're not talking about real life.

Lots of men fantasize total control of a

woman. They want to feel like potentates who can command their women to follow their every whim. It gives them a great feeling of might and strength to imagine their women are slaves to their simplest desires.

I know a woman who gets turned on by tickling. She imagines she's being tickled by her husband, and this feeling of losing control really excites her. Her husband hasn't a clue to what's going on in her mind.

And I know a man who visualizes himself crawling on his hands and knees in front of his wife, and this feeling of subservience turns *him* on. He doesn't want his wife to know, because he's hesitant that she might think it weak of him. He happens to be a good friend of mine, a very strong, good-looking man in show biz who let down his guard with me and "told all." I told him I believed he should share this with his wife, that that might turn him on even more, and he said he probably will—he's just not quite ready yet. But if he doesn't ever tell her, if he keeps it to himself, that's okay, too.

I could list a lot of different fantasies, but the

whole point is to make up your own. *You* know you have strong feelings and desires—and you *also* have a strong imagination.

USE IT!

Like a muscle, it gets stronger with use. And your own personal fantasies will get even more fantastic!

The beauty part of fantasies is that you can interchange them. One day you can be a powerful person, commanding and vigorous—a real martinet—and the next day you can be a weak person, reveling in your own weakness—helpless, defenseless, and *very* sexy in your helplessness. Or if power *really* turns you on, or weakness does, use one or the other *all* the time.

It's easy, it's fun, it hurts no one, and it just might add spice to your already terrific sex life.

Just remember—in fantasies, *anything* goes!!!

7
A Healthy Body

You might wonder why I've included a chapter on physical health in a book about sex. Again, I'm a very logical person, and when I explain it, you'll see how important health is to sex.

We may fall in love mentally or emotionally or spiritually—mentally you observe someone and you think you like what you see—a great smile, sensational legs, gorgeous eyes, an incredible body. Your thought processes race along and you decide to further pursue this person. Then your emotions begin to function—feelings begin to play within you which start urging you to get to really know this person. And spiritually you feel that this may be the missing half of your self for which you've been so eagerly searching for such a long time.

But all these thoughts and feelings and longings can't happen without a body, and cannot be fulfilled without a body. Without your body you can't think, you can't feel, and you can't desire. Your body is the vessel, the instrument, through which all of these things are expressed. Your body is truly the temple of God, although God knows most of us don't treat it so religiously. Most of us brutally mistreat our selves until it's a wonder we can function at all. No wonder we have a problem thinking straight—our veins and arteries are so clogged from eating junk and smoking and drinking booze, that oxygen has a hard time reaching our brains, so how is it *possible* to think clearly? After all, our brain is very much like an IBM machine. And when your body is full of tension or in the depths of a depression, you jam your computer, and you can't think clearly.

And the same for your emotions. When you're filled with tension and anxiety, it's impossible to be a loving person. It's not that you don't *want* to be sweet and caring and full of tenderness, you literally *cannot*. When you're tense and anxious, you hit your kids and scream at your husband or wife. You don't want to—you just can't help your self. And when you're depressed, you're sure not thrilled about hugging and kissing and making nice. You're probably thinking about how you can do away with your self.

So an unhealthy body is not a loving body. But the reverse is certainly true. A *really* healthy body is a loving body.

Sex is a normal function, like eating, drinking, walking, and sleeping. Now you don't feel like eating or drinking when you're sick, and you don't want to walk or move when you're sick, and certainly you don't sleep well when you're sick, and of course you don't want sex when you're sick.

When you're on drugs (cocaine, grass, booze, cigs, coffee, tea, etc.), you can usually eat and drink, though not well. You can usually walk, but not with a bounce in your step, and you can usually sleep, though fitfully. But drugs almost *always* interfere with your sex life.

Sex is one of the best barometers of health that there is. And this goes for both men and women. When a person is a heavy smoker (or even a moderate one), it negatively affects the sex organs. When a man or woman is sexually excited, the sex organs (penis and clitoris) engorge with blood and that's what excites us.

Smoking constricts all the veins and arteries in the body, particularly those in the sex organs, so they can't fill up with blood. This is what we call impotent—a sex organ that won't or can't fill with blood and therefore can't get hard.

And drinking too much booze will deplete the body of all the B vites, which are what keep the nervous system in good shape and keep us relaxed and sensual. So drinking booze will initially make us feel good for a few minutes, and then, as the effects wear off, it makes us tense, and we alternate between bouts of depression and anxiety, which feelings are not conducive to love and sex. Indeed, it will chase away any feelings or thoughts you might have had about making love. And coffee will do the same thing. It gives you a temporary "up," then plummets you down, so you need another cup, and another, till your body is so tense and anxious that love and sex are the last things on your mind. And so it goes with all the drugs—cocaine, grass, etc. They're all the same.

Of course, when we smoke or drink too much (women as well as men), it harms lots of *other* parts of our bodies, too, like our lungs, our liver, our heart, our skin, etc., but a *real* barometer of the harm done (and a quicker one) is our sex life. When we smoke, the nicotine constricts our blood vessels (it really makes them a *lot* smaller), and as I said, the swelling of the blood vessels is the cause of erection and sexual excitement in both men and women. And the inhaled carbon monoxide reduces the level of blood-oxygen and also the hormone production.

When a person is a heavy smoker, the lung capacity is cut *way* down, and that cuts *way* down on your endurance and on the ability to last a while during intercourse. Try it. See what happens when you cut out the smokes for a month. If your sex life doesn't pick up considerably (and I mean your ability as a lover), then you can always go back to smoking. I know it's difficult to stop, but if I did it, anyone can.

One of the wonderful things about life is that things are usually never totally lost. There is usually hope that something can be salvaged. The good news about stopping smoking is that once a person stops, the body is totally cleared of all the tar and nicotine and assorted gunk in a matter of months. Several doctors have told me that people should never feel that because they've been smoking for years it wouldn't make any difference if they stop—that all the damage has already been done; that's simply not true. Your lungs will go back to their pre-smoking condition a few months after you stop.

Alcoholism is a result of nutritional deficiencies (particularly the B vites), so, because our bodies are malnourished, we crave liquor—which makes our bodies more nutritionally deficient, and we become more malnourished, and we crave more booze, etc., etc., etc.

So the main thing to do for men who want to have a super sex life is to cut down the booze, cut out the smokes altogether, and start exercising those gorgeous bodies and getting them in shape. Jogging is a terrific way to begin, even if it's running in place in your bedroom. Once you see how good you're feeling, you might even graduate to running outside.

Now I'm sure some men smoke and drink too much and still function well, but believe me, they are the exception. And their sexual prowess won't (can't) last. These men start out in life in better shape than most of us, so it takes the nicotine and booze a little while longer to get to them. But get they will.

And as important as it is for *men* to be in great shape physically to be terrific lovers, it's important for women, too. The clitoris is a miniature penis, and if a woman puts gunk in her body, her clit will react exactly the same as a man's penis—it will be difficult, if not impossible, to keep it erect, and she will lose her desire for sex.

Remember, it's *impossible* to keep an erection if your body isn't healthy—it's *not* a mental problem where you can *will* or *demand* your penis to be hard, and it's not an emotional problem where a new and exciting bed partner will stimulate you, and your penis will automatically get hard—it's a *physical* problem if you're mistreating your body by loading it with junk and booze and cigs and other drugs. Your penis *cannot* get hard until you change your self and get healthy.

Once you get your physical self in great shape, and your mental self sharpens up (which it *will* when your body is activated), and your emotional self softens and expands as the love increases in your life, you'll find the life forces growing greatly in every part of your physical, mental, and emotional self. The ultimate expression of this life force is sex—a juicy, delicious, loving, and exciting sex life. This is only *one* of the ways of pleasuring your self, but it is the ultimate.

The great turn-on for sex is love, and love is what this book is all about. When you have love radiating from every pore, and love surrounding every thought, and love filling every passion, then you'll know what life is *supposed* to be.

So work at getting healthy and I promise you

you'll feel better than you've ever felt.

People are so used to feeling tense and anxious that they think it's a natural way of life—that that's the way they're *supposed* to feel. Only after they've gotten rid of tension and anxiety do they realize how awful they *used* to feel and how unnatural it is to feel that awful.

The natural way to feel is calm and relaxed yet full of energy, waking up in the morning wanting to take over the world. That's what life is *supposed* to be like. But most people don't feel that good, and I sure didn't either. I used to be so full of tension and anxiety that I couldn't function, then I'd fall into the pits of depression. I used to think my fears and depressions were all mental, so I tried everything—yoga, psychologists, psychiatrists, meditation—but let me tell you, you can meditate for ten months, or see a shrink for six years, and if your body's screaming out with tension, nothing mental is going to help.

On the other hand, when your body is feeling super good, you'll start thinking more clearly than you ever did before—you'll find you don't get confused anymore. And you'll be amazed at how your personal relationships will improve. People will find you more relaxed and more loving—because when you're relaxed you won't yell at your kids, kick the cat, or pick fights with your mate.

So the very first step is to get rid of all the physical tension in your body, and I've found the all-time best way to do this. Only a person who's felt as low and really awful as I used to feel can understand why I'm so grateful for the great change that happened to me several years ago. Anything that could change my life so drastically, that could make me feel so incredibly good every day, is a miracle.

Now everyone who's read two of my books, *Everything You've Always Wanted to Know About Energy . . . But Were too Weak to Ask,* and *Isle of View (Say It Out Loud),* knows a little about how I changed my life, but I'd like to tell my new readers how it happened. If through my experience I can help even one person to feel better, that will make me very happy.

Before my wonderful discovery, I was a

wreck on my ten cups a day (at least) of coffee, my pack a day (at least) of cigarettes, and so many sweets I can't believe I was even alive, let alone functioning. I was tense and anxious between my bouts of depression. Every day I smoked and drank coffee and tea and colas and ate candy and cakes to whip myself into action. Then I'd have a martini to relax at the end of the day, then coffee, cigs, and sweets after dinner to push my self again, and then to bed where I slept horribly, with lots of nightmares, and the next day the same routine all over again.

Finally, I had a physical collapse—my body just conked out. They took me to the hospital where the doctors thought I had mono or a kidney disease—and at the time I was very young, in my early twenties. While I was in the hospital, a friend, Rachel Perry, gave me one of Adelle Davis's books and I found out that all the things which I'd had wrong with me physically since I was a little kid came from tension, which was caused by a lack of the B vitamins. I later found out that the B vites in my body were being used up by all the sugar and junk I was eating.

Sugar, to be metabolized, burns up all the B vites in the metabolic process. No wonder I was such a wreck!

Then I found out that yeast is the most concentrated source of all the B vites in any food, and those B vites could also knock out tension and depression—so that's when I invented my Dynamite Energy Shake. Not only did the canker sores and neuralgia attacks and pimples go away, but the tension just sort of drained out of my body, and my depressions faded away. I could feel them leaving and a wonderful sense of well-being taking over.

At that time I made my Dynamite Energy Shake from scratch, but now you can buy it ready-made at all health stores, or to order direct, call 1-800-255-1660, M–F, 9:30–5:30 e.s.t. I worked months perfecting the formula so that it would not only make you feel sensational, but would also taste terrific.

I'm so grateful that God gave me my physical collapse that led to my inventing the Dynamite Energy Shake, that I decided to put all the money that would have come to me from the sale of the Dynamite Energy Shake, every penny, into a foundation—The John Ellsworth Hayden Foundation—that I named after my father. The foundation is giving free Dynamite Energy Shakes to people who can't afford it or who wouldn't be able to get it otherwise. I want to give it to every prison I can get it into, because I truly believe that some people commit crimes because of nutritional deficiencies that lead to tension. The same way people drink to escape tension and some fight with their mates and kids and friends as a result of tension, some other people who have chemically imbalanced bodies and serious nutritional deficiencies commit crimes because of the tension.

Free Dynamite Energy Shakes are also going to those people in mental institutes, senior citizens' homes, and other places where there are people whom I feel could be benefited enormously by putting something this potent in their bodies, something that could change thier physical, mental, and emotional lives.

In my *Energy* and *Isle of View* books I give the real basics about vitamins, but I'd like to tell you just a little here about why you need them and how many you should take. If you want to find out a lot *more* of the details of vitamins and the Dynamite Energy Shake, read both of my previous books. I've made it *really* logical and simple and easy to understand.

Before I found out about vitamins, I was as confused as everybody else about how many to take and which ones I needed. I used to take a multivitamin once a day, and thought I was getting everything I needed, but now that I've studied and found out a lot about vites, I know I wasn't getting anywhere *near* as many as I needed.

Every body is individual and has individual needs. We don't all need the same amount of vites. What I've done is list what I believe is the *minimum* for *every body* (I take much more, which I list under the minimums). Some of you may need just the minimum, and others may need more like I do, but I'll tell you how you will know if you're getting enough or need more.

LIST OF VITAMINS AND MINERALS

MINIMUM TO TAKE DAILY*

Vitamin A—25,000 units
All the B Vitamins—Get plenty in Dynamite
Energy Shake
Vitamin C—3,000 mgs.
Vitamin D—3,000 units
Vitamin E—400 units
Dolomite—1,300 mgs. (10 pills or 1 level tsp.
powder)
Other Minerals—Get plenty in Dynamite
Energy Shake

WHAT I TAKE DAILY

Vitamin A—50,000 units
All the B Vitamins—Get plenty in Dynamite
Energy Shake
Vitamin C—15,000 mgs.
Vitamin D—3,000 units
Vitamin E—3,600 units
Dolomite—3,900 mgs. 30 pills or 3 level tsp.
powder
Other Minerals—Get plenty in Dynamite
Energy Shake

*Give children proportionately less according to their body weight.
For instance, a twelve year old who weighs 100 lbs, give ¾ of amounts
listed, a five year old who weighs 50 lbs, give ¼ of amounts listed, etc.
Give Vit. C according to frequency of colds, etc. the child gets.

Let's start with Vitamin A. Vitamin A is essential to good skin—it prevents and clears up skin infections. It also makes hair shiny, improves day vision and particularly night vision, promotes cell growth, and aids in resisting infections.

Vitamin A and Vitamin E work together and should be taken together, because without Vitamin E, Vitamin A is destroyed by oxygen. Vitamin A is found in green and yellow vegetables and apricots. The National Research Council recommends 5,000 units a day, but I take 50,000 units a day, and I believe that 25,000 units a day should be a minimum for an adult.

The B vitamins are B_1, B_2, B_6, B_{12}, biotin, folic acid, inositol, niacin, pantothenic acid, and PABA (para amino benzoic acid). Science is finding there are other B vites, and has recently isolated two, B_{16} (pangamic acid) and B_{17} (amygdalin). All the B vites are water-soluble and can't be stored in the body, so they must be taken every day. They are synergistic, which means that one alone or several together increase the need for the rest of them. For instance, if you took lots of B_1 or B_6, it could make you terribly deficient in all the other B's. When you take the Dynamite Energy Shake, you'll be getting *all* the B vites, and lots of them, because it's *loaded* with them.

Vitamin C is ascorbic acid, and Nobel Prize-winner Linus Pauling recommends at least 3,000 mgs a day, but I take a minimum of 15,000 mgs a day and have for years. If I start to sneeze or feel a cold coming on, I go up to 50,000 mgs a day, and several times have taken as much as 100,000 mgs in a day, but each time I knocked the virus out that same day, and can honestly say that since I've been on high doses of Vitamin C, *I haven't been sick even one day* (and I used to get colds and flu bugs and viruses maybe eight or ten times a year, bedding me each time for a couple of days—and my doctor bills and antibiotic bills were enormous). Vitamin C is fantastic, but you do need massive doses (always taken with a *lot* of liquid). *If you're taking Vitamin C and still get a cold, then know that you're not taking enough.* And continue taking the large amount of C for at least a day after you start to feel you're all better (and you generally *do* start to feel better right away after taking a lot of C), because if you stop too soon, the germs will begin to multiply again.

If you have bleeding gums or bruises on your body, these are signs of a Vitamin C deficiency. If you never get a cold or flu bug, then you probably need far less than the rest of us, and 3,000 or 4,000 mgs a day should be enough for you. Vitamin C is water-soluble and can't be stored in the body, so any excess is flushed out, and the body tissues should be saturated with it every day. Again, be sure to drink lots of liquids when you take lots of Vitamin C. Just use your body as a barometer: If you feel great and don't catch colds or viruses, then 3,000 mg a day is enough—if you do catch colds, etc., then you need more.

Vitamin D is known as the sunshine vitamin and helps the body absorb calcium and retain it. Without Vitamin D, much calcium is lost. Foods don't contain much, so many people are terribly deficient and don't know why they are so nervous. Vitamin D cannot be absorbed without fat or oil, so take it after a meal that includes some oil. Vitamin D, like Vitamin A, can be toxic, but only in massive doses. I take two packets of my own vitamins every day, which give me 3,000 units of Vitamin D, or 21,000 units a week. Dr. J.A. Johnston of the Henry Ford Hospital in Detroit researched Vitamin D, and his studies show that an adult can profit by taking at least 4,000 units daily, and even though I take only 3,000 units a day (21,000 a week) in my vitamins, I get more in the eggs I eat and the milk I drink every day. Of course, I also try to get a *little* sunshine every day just walking around.

Vitamin E is an oxygenizer and it helps all the muscles in the body by lowering the needs for oxygen. With more oxygen, the heart doesn't have to work as hard. Vitamin E is sometimes called the sex vitamin, and helps produce normal sex hormones. Vitamin E also adds oxygen to the brain and has been used to help mentally retarded children. Dr. Del Giudice, head of child psychology at the National Institute of Public Health in Buenos Aires, Argentina, has given mentally retarded children 2,000 to 3,000 units of Vitamin E daily for many years with surprisingly successful results, and no evidence of toxicity. If you have high blood pressure, I suggest you start *very* slowly with 100 units of Vitamin E, and after you've been on the shake and vites and have gotten healthier and your blood pressure has lowered, then up your Vitamin E to 400 units. Most everyone else should begin with 800 units, or if you want to start slowly, 400 units and build up to 800. I take 3,600 units a day now and feel great.

Dolomite contains calcium and magnesium, both super-important for your nerves. It comes in pills and powder. A teaspoon of powder in milk or juice or even water (it's tasteless) is equivalent to about ten pills, and ten pills is about the equivalent of the calcium in a quart of milk. If you're under a lot of stress (and who isn't nowadays?), take at least ten pills a day (or one teaspoon powder in liquid). I usually take thirty-six pills a day, but with all the things I'm doing, I really need 'em to keep me cool. Dolomite is a great natural tranquilizer. It's also awfully important for older people who usually don't get enough calcium and whose bones are getting brittle and porous. It will not only strengthen your bones and keep them from breaking, it'll also calm those frazzled nerves.

To me one of the saddest and most ridiculous things about MDRs (minimum daily requirements) put out by Washington and used by countless doctors all over the country, is the MDR on Vitamin C, which is 60 mgs. According to the statistics, 60 mgs of Vitamin C will keep you from getting scurvy, which disease marks the last stage of a Vitamin C deficiency before you *die!* That's like saying the MDR of water is two ounces a day, that that will keep you from dying from a lack of water (or dehydration). Now obviously one wants to be healthier than a borderline case of scurvy which is one step from death, and the sad part is that so many people accept the MDRs as gospel, and are starving their poor bodies from a lack of vitamins, and so many ignorant doctors promote the MDRs as the last word on nutrition. There are lots of great doctors in the world and there are lots of close-minded ones. If you're wise, you'll search out the ones who are open-minded, who are constantly learning about new findings, and who are into preventive medicine and nutrition.

Just try to remember that vitamins are foods, not drugs. It always astounds me how some doctors warn people about taking vitamins, which are foods and promote great health, and they don't warn people about drinking coffee or tea or colas or eating sugar, all of which are addictive. Once you become aware of your body and listen to what it's telling you, you'll become more sensitive to what it needs and what to put in and what to keep out. And once you *do* get to know your self physically, and your body starts to feel really healthy, you'll begin to know your self mentally and emotionally, too. That's the basis of happiness, because when you *really* know your self, you can get rid of all the negative things and cultivate all the positive things. That's when you'll begin to like your self, and life will begin to be fun and exciting.

The shakes and vites are not a diet—they're a way of life. They become as much a habit as brushing your teeth every day. Everything you put in your body is a cause and will have an effect—some right away, like pimples, head-aches, canker sores—and some are long-term effects, like strokes, ulcers, heart attacks. When you abuse your gorgeous body (well, it *will* be when you take care of it), you really can't blame it when it starts to fall apart. But the wonderful thing is that *it's never too late to change.* So even if you've been doing wrong things for years, you can now start a new way of life, one that will make you healthier and happier.

The Dynamite Energy Shake and vites changed my life completely. Now I'm the health-iest, most energetic person I know, and I want *every body* to feel as good as I do!

8
Living Alone

What do you do about sex if you're living alone? Your wife died several years ago. Your fella is in the service overseas and won't be back for another year. Your girlfriend has dumped you. You decided you would be better off divorced, so you and husby split several months ago.

All right, now you're alone and whether you like it or not is irrelevant. You're trying to make the best of it and you're coping pretty well. Except for sex—or the lack of it. When you had a partner, a mate, you may have fought like crazy, but you were at least with another warm-blooded human being. Because the relationship was so strained, there wasn't a lot of love floating around, but at least there was occasional sex. And as they say, "At its worst it's better than anything else."

Well, I believe God gave us sex organs for a reason. And I believe in sex with love. And preferably sex with love in marriage. But if that isn't possible, I don't believe God meant for us to be celibate.

In his book *Sex Can Save Your Heart and Life,* Dr. Eugene Scheimann points out that celibacy just about destroyed earlier civilization, and that some scholars believe that celibacy, not orgies, led to the decline and fall of the Roman Empire:

> "During the early centuries, the Christians actually tried to get rid of sex entirely. . . . It wasn't Christ's idea, nor that of his earliest followers with the possible exception of Saint Paul, but his later followers became obsessed with stamping out sex. . . . Over the years, this attitude took its toll. The

glorification of celibacy led to a decline in the population of the Western Empire. The defeat of Rome by the barbarian Huns from the North has been blamed on everything from decadence to lead poisoning, but one scholar, Dr. Richard Lewinsohn, claims that the antisex doctrine was responsible. 'Unless we can assume that the innumerable treatises in favor of asceticism were mere literary efforts and that no one except a few thousand monks and nuns ordered their lives after them, one is forced to conclude that sexual abstinence did more [than corruption] to bring about the downfall of Rome.' "

Again, sex is a natural function just like eating, drinking, walking, and sleeping. Just as you hopefully don't glut your body by gorging with food or drink till your belly juts out, you also hopefully don't starve your body of nutrients, or keep your self from drinking liquids till you're all shriveled from thirst.

All appetites are meant to be satisfied. Not

gorged and not starved. A happy medium. We use self-control. Someone may give you a gorgeous strawberry mousse cake, but that doesn't mean you dive in and eat the whole thing in one sitting. That would undoubtedly make you sick. A small slice after dinner, another small slice tomorrow. With care, it could last a week or two.

The same with sex. It's certainly all around us, and it's not too difficult to come by nowadays. But just to grab the first available body is not the answer. In fact, that will probably disgust your self with your self, and could turn you off sex *altogether* for a while.

Now if you're a healthy person, you're going to have a healthy sex drive. You didn't ask for it. You were born with it. *All* healthy persons have healthy sex drives. It makes no difference if you're a priest, nun, schoolteacher, postman, race-car driver, movie star, astronaut, or attorney. If you're healthy, it's there. Some of us may try to sublimate it in religious activities, or sports, or an artistic endeavor. But it's still there. And wishing won't make it go away.

Again, Dr. Eugene Scheimann says:

"Freud was not the first doctor to notice that people who got sick often had severe sex problems. But Freud was the first to make this a subject for science. . . His theories became the basis of psychiatry, and the foundation of psychosomatic medicine . . . he demonstrated that when sexual desires are repressed into the unconscious, they often show up, not only in dreams and accidents and psychological upsets, but in organic disease. . . Recent insights into human sexuality seem to suggest that not only was he on the right track, but that in truth he didn't go far enough."

So what to do without a partner. Well, there are pros and cons to self-satisfaction. Michael, a character in Mart Crowley's Off-Broadway play *The Boys In The Band,* believes it cuts down your wardrobe needs. He says, "Well, one thing you can say for masturbation—you certainly don't have to look your best." Some people believe in it and do it all the time, and others are offended by the mere mention of it. I personally think that anything in life that doesn't hurt you in any way physically, mentally, or emotionally, or doesn't hurt anyone else physically, mentally, or emotionally, and is pleasure-full and feels good and is health-full and is good for your circulation and well-being, *must* be good.

But if you feel that something—*anything*—is not good for you, and that thing—whatever it is—makes you feel guilty, then I don't think you should do it. This goes for food that you eat, liquids that you drink, actions that you make, and sex.

I believe sex should always be with love, but then I believe that *everything* should be done with love. What is love? It's caring—caring about your self, your family, your friends, your pets, your plants. And what is caring? Taking care of. So to love is to take care of. When you truly love your self, you take care of your self—you take care that you put only health-full foods and health-full drinks into your body, and only health-full thoughts and feelings into your mind. Love is all-pervasive.

And if you're living alone, either through circumstance or through choice, love should be in every part of *your* life, too. You have no one to take care of but your self, and you have no one to take care of *you* but your self, so *you* have to care for your self. Caring is love and love is caring.

You should care for and pleasure your self in every possible way that makes you feel good physically, mentally, and emotionally.

In the *Redbook* survey is this report:

"The activity once thought to cause warts is now recommended to do all but cure them . . . therapists advise masturbation to survive sexually without a partner."

In *Sexual Confidence,* Dr. Debora Phillips says:

"The list of bad things about masturbation can be summed up in a word: Nothing. Except the attitude that masturbation is shameful.

Masturbation is a pleasure. And human beings are especially endowed with a great capacity for pleasure. The woman's clitoris, for example, has nothing to do with procreation. The only function a clitoris has is to give pleasure. Isn't it remarkable that we humans have been given an organ that is only for sexual pleasure?"

Dr. Phillips goes on:

"The Reverend Dr. William Kirby, a Protestant theologian, states, 'Let's start with love. Is sex loving? Sex before or after marriage or between two individuals of the same or different sex cannot simply be placed into a category of good or bad or wrong or right or liberating or confining, but rather whether it is loving.'"

Then she adds:

"Theologian and author Rabbi Reeve Brenner points out: 'To Jews, sex is a blessing . . . In the Hebrew Bible (the Old Testament) and in the Talmud, Judaism makes a strong argument *against* celibacy and *for* the raptures of love.'"

If you've found the love of your life and you have a great relationship, you're a lucky person—but if you haven't, don't deny your self pleasure. Certainly love is the all-time greatest pleasure in the world, but love comes in many packages. I believe in feeling good so long as you don't hurt your self or anyone else. The only possible thing that could hurt you is guilt, and if you're a loving person who's actively spreading love, there's nothing to be guilty about.

Pleasure your self as much and as often as you can. Eat wholesome food, breathe clean, fresh air, drink lots of pure water, use all your muscles, take good care of your skin and your body. Do as many of the things that you can do to make your self feel better physically, mentally, and emotionally.

9
The Joy of Marriage

Now we come to my favorite subject, marriage. I don't believe in living together—"playing house"—and I truly believe in the commitment of marriage. I think it's the greatest relationship that two people can ever have. A partnership with someone who loves you. What could be better?

I also believe strongly, as I stated earlier, in faithfulness in marriage. I don't think you can break the bond of trust in a marriage without seriously damaging the relationship. And I don't mean that he'll find out she's fooling around, or she'll catch him with another woman. I mean the person who's *cheating* will feel damaged. *That*

111

person will know the trust is broken, and the relationship can never be the same.

I hate it when a married man makes a play for me. Even if he's the handsomest, darlingest man-about-town, it truly distresses me. I don't want him to embarrass his wife by flirting outrageously with me or any other woman.

And I'm *really* happy when a married man is attentive to his wife and acts like he's in love, and doesn't make goo-goo eyes at me or anyone else.

That might seem strange, you might think I would *love* any male attention, but again for Naura's logic. A man who pays attention to his wife, who is polite and gracious but doesn't single out or flirt with other women, proves to me that it *is* possible to find a man who will be faithful, who won't fool around, and who can be trusted. The married man who ignores his wife and flirts with me would flirt with other women *exactly* the same way if he were married to me.

I want a man who loves me and who is faithful *because* of his love and devotion and trust and all those other beautiful feelings that we all have but don't always use.

So why do so many people fool around outside of marriage? Why is it thousands and thousands of marriages are broken up every day? Why do families split, destroying children's emotional lives and traumatizing the broken partners?

I believe most of it stems from incomplete sex lives. Most women are faking orgasms and are deeply dissatisfied sexually with their husbands and their marriages, and are looking around for "Mr. Right" to fulfill them in this very important way.

And the men fooling around are doing it because they sense their wives are not *deeply* in love with them, and all men, like all women, are searching for a deep emotional love. *Deep* love comes only when both partners are united heart-to-heart, soul-to-soul, and body-to-body.

Now I've heard lots of people say that sex isn't everything, and that it's overstated in a relationship. People have told me that companionship and compatibility are what really count, and that sex isn't *that* important or necessary for a happy marriage, and also that many marriages are just as happy without it.

I *totally* disagree with this.

To me, being married and living together without sex is like cooking a super-delectable seven course dinner and saying, "You can look at it, you can touch it, you can smell it, you can taste it, but you *can't* eat it!"

You can be married and compatible and love to do all the same kinds of things together, but without sex, your union is not complete. And anyone who says it is has obviously got problems in his or her sex life, and the marriage can't be a really happy and complete one.

Of *course*, companionship is important in a relationship, very important. And having things in common is what makes you so compatible. The fact that you both love movies and hate picnics, or adore dancing and loathe golf, is part of what makes being together fun. But sex is one of the strongest and most important feelings we have in life—physically, mentally, and emotionally. And to underestimate it is a foolish and dangerous thing to do, because that might lead you to overlook unhappiness in the boudoir, instead of looking for solutions.

Sure, other things are important, but don't ever forget that sex is the *closest* two people can get. Certainly physically (you literally can't *get* any closer!), but also there is a bond formed mentally and emotionally when sexual pleasuring is the ultimate joy for both partners.

I believe God gave us our sex organs so that we would be bonded to each other in pleasure *forever* within marriage. Sex was also given to us for procreation. But if this were *all* it was for, sexual feelings would then cease when a woman can't procreate, or when a man is unable to have children. And they don't.

If a man and woman are *truly* sexually happy together, there would be no reason for him or her to look elsewhere for sex. When a man and woman love each other and share the joy of ecstasy when they express their love in sex, why *would* they look around?

A truly sad story I read a few years ago was told by a woman doctor in her eighties who had been very happily married right after the turn of the century. She was deeply in love with her husband, another doctor, who loved her just as deeply. She told how one night at the beginning of their marriage they made love and she experienced the most incredible feeling of ecstasy that she had ever felt, a feeling of her body exploding and expanding into space. Much later, she learned that what she had experienced was an orgasm. At that time, however, the ecstasy of the feeling was *so* intense that it frightened her and her husband to the extent that in later sex relations she tensed up physically to keep herself from any further enjoyment of her husband's body-union with her. They were both taught that a woman did not enjoy sex, that any pleasure in the sex act was forbidden for a woman.

She related how he died a few years later, and when she finally realized that her ecstasy with her mate was a beautiful and tender part of their love, something to be cherished, not feared, and that she had stopped it—she had actually *killed* all the physical joy and passion with the man she totally loved—her regret was so profound that it filled her with a sadness that she could never shake for the rest of her life.

How lucky we are today to be living in an era of openness in so many areas. Men and women today are frank in their discussions of sex. Years ago, when there was so much shame and guilt, no *wonder* THE BIG BANG got started. Wham, bam, thank you ma'am. Just do it fast and hard and get it over with. No wonder women (and men) have had so many sexual problems through the years. Shame and guilt are *awful* bedfellows.

A great part of great love, a very, *very* important part, is expressing that love through sex. You hear about so many couples having unhappy sex lives because the wife isn't satisfied. I was in Salt Lake City recently and a friend was telling me about some problems in his marriage. He said their sex life was awful and his wife didn't ever really enjoy sex. They're both in their twenties, and deeply religious Mormons. I explained to him about THE BIG BANG THEORY and suggested he follow my advice at least once and see what would happen. He called me the next week in New York and said his wife had had her first orgasm and was a different woman. His happiness floated right through the phone.

Helen Gurley Brown is a truly beautiful woman, inside and out, and loaded with sex appeal. I'll never forget a couple of years ago when we both were on the same plane from New York to Los Angeles. She got up to stretch her legs, and every man on the plane craned his neck to watch her as she reached for her bag and then headed for the restroom. When I saw her later in Los Angeles at the baggage claim, I told her of all the men eyeing her, and asked her how does she keep so sexy all the time? She gave me a great reply which I could *never* forget. Helen said she feels so much love from her husband, David, and that it's *with* her all the time, and it makes her *feel* sexy all the time. Wow! Now *there's* a great love affair *and* a great marriage.

A few years ago I created a phrase: "Pay attention instead of alimony."

Alimony is expensive (for men *and* women!). Attention isn't.

Attention is a pat on the fanny, a "you look great!", and even a simple "I love you," and if you have trouble saying *that*, say "Isle of View" (from the book of the same name)!

Attention is taking your spouse's hand while walking down the street, winking across a crowded cocktail party, calling long distance the night you arrive across the country and saying "I just wanted you to know I miss you."

Attention is a lot of things. A lot of simple things. But most importantly it's letting your mate know you care. You care how he feels. You care how she looks. You care what he eats and drinks. You care that she keeps healthy.

Caring is loving. Loving is caring.

I never met Hubert Humphrey, but he was a good friend of someone very close to me, who tells of Hubie's great love and devotion and pride in his wife, Muriel. He invited my friend to Minneapolis many times to have dinner so that Muriel could make her famous vegetable soup. "Muriel makes the best vegetable soup in America," he said, *so* many times that even if she didn't, everyone was convinced that she could out-cook L'Escoffier. Hubert was a devoted, attentive husband who had a wonderful marriage because he not only loved his wife, he made sure she knew it. He made her a big part of his life (and that isn't always easy in politics!).

The few people I know who have happy relationships *all* pay attention instead of alimony. They have learned that the greatest joy in the whole world is to be deeply loved and cared for and pleasured sexually by your mate.

This is *truly* the joy of marriage.

And the joy of marriage is *truly* the joy of life!

A Married Man's Incredible Letter to Me . . .

I have received tens of thousands of letters since my book came out in 1983, and I cannot tell you how thrilling it is for me to know that my book has saved so many marriages, and made so many other marriages happier than they ever thought possible.

Some are from couples who tell me they were going to marriage counselors, and some of them were cheating on each other, but after using the technique, *all* said they were closer and happier than ever, and now totally monogamous.

Others are from wives telling me they had never had an orgasm before they and their husbands read the book.

Others are from husbands saying they never felt so much love from their wives as now since they learned how to intercourse correctly.

Still others told me they were actually in the process of getting a divorce when the husband or wife got my book, got the spouse to read it, and changed their whole lives around with more emotional intimacy than they ever dreamed possible.

But the most incredible letter I *ever* received arrived in November of 1991 from a man in Virginia who sent me 14 handwritten pages (he says at the end that he obviously couldn't have had his secretary type it), and it is such a sincere and loving letter from a husband who obviously really loves his wife of 18 years that I was genuinely moved by it.

He tells how upset and frustrated he was by her lack of responsiveness and pleasure in lovemaking during their years together, so much so that he contemplated cheating on her and even thought about the possibility of divorce.

He says my book changed his life and his marriage . . .

11/18/91 7:19 A.M.

Dear Naura :

I've never written to an author before.
I've enjoyed alot of books and some
have moved me, some changed me and
some have taught me something. But I've
never had a book change my life before.
Over this past weekend I was driving my
son (13) to a soccer tournament. He
was asleep in the back of the van and
it was probably 10:30 at night. I
found I was trying to find a
radio station to keep me awake. I still
had 100 miles to go. I heard your
interview on your book How To Satisfy a
Woman Every Time and somehow knew you
were onto something.

My wife and I have been married for
18 years. In that time she has probably
had 18 orgasms. She never liked
oral sex; said it tickled too much.
Manual manipulation was OK up to
a point, she'd get excited and want me
to put my penis inside her, NOW!
Over the years I've read all variety
of sex books trying to find a way to
help her achieve orgasm. We ended up
fighting over sex because I felt she
was frigid because of a horrible

123

relationship with her stepfather.
She has told me how afraid of him
she was — that she was always afraid
to be alone with him because of sexual
comments. I believe he probably sexually
abused her but she has never been able
to admit this, perhaps not even to
herself. He certainly did severe
emotional damage to her and I believed
this was why she was "frigid". In the final
analysis, I felt she was afraid to let herself orgasm.

She and I even went to a sex therapist
(psychologist) for a while but that did no
good. I just wanted her to feel good
sexually & that I could make her feel
good. I'll certainly admit that it was
a real ego blow for me that I couldn't
help my wife achieve orgasm more than once
a year. I know she did reach orgasm once
a year (approximately) because she never
faked it. Her most telling statements
in that time were: "there's nothing
wrong with me, I just don't have
orgasms very often, I just can't relax
enough, you'll just have to accept me
as I am." Those words have rung in
my ears for years and I felt totally
helpless to do anything about it because
she gave up wanting to try.

124

She hated to talk about sex, and although she promised to read the occasional therapy book I brought home, she never did.

Interestingly, she was the one that always hurried sex. Foreplay was very short — she said it tickled too much and just wanted me in her. I don't think it was just to get it over with because foreplay was so short I wasn't sufficiently aroused ~~for me to~~ for me to come quickly.

It's also important to note that I have been so frustrated by "her" lack of responsiveness in passing that I have contemplated divorce many times believing I would be happier with a "sexually responsive" woman. Sex has become less frequent in recent years because she's too tired, not feeling good, etc. I always have felt that if she could achieve orgasm more often she would be more interested (now, I'll get to find out, but more about that later.)

That night on the radio, although you weren't explicit about your technique, your sincerity told me you knew what you were talking about. While driving 70 mph down the highway I managed to write your name, 800 # and

125

and the name of the book. And I even managed to avoid running off the road.

The next morning in Roanoke, VA I got to a book store, sent my son off to the young adult section, found your book, (it was hard to find, it's so small) and bought it immediately. We then went off to the soccer tournament, (the kids won both games) and returned to the motel room. While the soccer team was playing outside,

waiting for the parents to take them to dinner, I read your book and I knew you were right. I couldn't wait to get home to see my wife. I was concerned because I wanted her to read your book. I felt she would not want to do so based on past experience. I was also concerned she would feel threatened by bringing up the subject, yet once again. And although I felt I could try your approach even without her knowledge, I felt it would be easier, better, etc. if she knew what was going on, particularly with her history of wanting to rush through foreplay because it tickled too much. Interestingly I had tried your method previously but had always allowed her to pull me all the way in after a minute or two. She thought she wanted ~~that~~ me to be all the way in and I thought she did too. ~~It's~~ so sad that ~~⬤~~ allowing us both to give in to that was ~~so~~ self defeating.

Anyway, on to the main event. After the ~~tournament~~ my son & I drove home and I kept running through my mind ~~how~~ I would ~~approach~~ the subject of your book, methods, and get her to read it. We got the kids ~~to bed~~, cleaned up downstairs and went to bed ourselves. As she was changing I told her ~~about~~ your radio interview ~~and~~ that I had read your book and felt you were really onto something. I told her I wanted her to give me ~~a birthday~~ a birthday present. (I'll be 40, next week) I wanted her to read the book. She indicated she would, but once again I could hear in her voice, she had no intention of doing so. I think your book represented a threat. If she read it and we ~~tried~~ your techniques and they didn't work — once again she would have failed. Even ~~though~~ it wouldn't have been a failure on her part I must admit I would have silently blamed her and her background for her failure to achieve orgasm and based on

127

my blaming her, other ~~books~~ blaming her (a woman is responsible for her own ~~orgasm~~), and the sex therapist blaming her, I'm sure she must have ~~either~~ been blaming herself or hating the world when it came to the subject or both. *That's the other reason woman fake it. They think something is wrong with them.*

~forgosm

Anyway, I did not tell her anything about your techniques but wanted to let her curiosity to take over. I wasn't sure ~~it would~~ ~~work~~. She would read it regardless.

She then came over to my side of the bed to cuddle as she frequently does when she wants to make love. I began running my fingertips up and down her arm. She began to shiver, and said, "You know I don't like you to touch me that lightly, it tickles too much." I started rubbing her back the same way which she tolerated for a while but clearly was uncomfortable. She rolled over onto her back and she put my hand on her ~~x~~ still panty-clad vagina. She ~~apparently~~ figured she needed once again, to ~~speed~~ this whole thing up. She didn't want to be "tickled" anymore. ~~Instead,~~ I moved my hand up to her breast and started making slow light fingertip touch circles ~~about~~ her nipple. She held my hand ~~with which~~ I was caressing her ~~with,~~ ~~some~~ as ~~to~~ she always does, so she can pull my hand away when

128

she becomes too sensitive. Again, she tolerated the fingertip touch for about a minute, but again felt the need to speed things up. Because she could see I was in no hurry she pulled her panties off, pushed me onto my back and began to mount me. I felt defeated because as she lowered herself on me it was difficult for me to keep her out, with her on top. *How was I going to get her to read the Book?*

As I lay on my back I put my hands under her hips and kept her from ~~fully~~ being fully penetrated. She was frustrated by this but "tolerated" it for awhile because she knew I was up to something based on your book, she just couldn't figure out what. After a few minutes of this, she decided she'd had enough of this foolishness and pulled me over into the missionary position. NOW, I WAS IN CONTROL!

I pulled back and continually moved my penis into and around the opening of her vagina paying particular attention to the top and her clitoris. Slowly, gently, carefully probing never entering her more than with the head of my penis. We went on like this for 5 to 10 minutes and I could just feel her

129

excitement increasing. Her breathing
got ~~so~~ deeper and pronounced. A
few times she grabbed my hips and
tried to pull me all the way in but
I resisted her. She tensed and seemed almost
angry. I ignored this response and just
~~kep~~ kept going lightly, right at the rim.
Finally, (you're right!) she begged —
"please put it in!" And for the first time
I said gently but firmly (and with a fair
amount of self control) "no! not yet."

Now she understood, I could feel she
understood. I was in control of her,
and I was not going to enter her until
I was ready. She was getting more
intense feelings all the time and we
were going to continue just this way
until I decided to change it. It was
marvelous. Based on this new unspoken
understanding, I continued to tease her
for another few minutes. Then it happened,
she tried to pull me in one more time and I
wouldn't let her. Then she orgasmed. I
hadn't gotten to the ½", 1", 1½", 2" penetration
you suggested, I was still teasing at the opening
because I didn't want to lose control of the
situation, her or myself. I'll have to
work on that in the future.

ANYWAY, SHE ORGASMED! I was on cloud nine

She pulled me to her and I went
hungrily but carefully. She bucked and
her vagina and love stunned spasmed around
me in a way I had only felt a few times
previously. I came within a minute and
felt like a million, no ten million
dollars, (after taxes). I HAD DONE IT.
That's the funny part. I felt like she had to
and know something
incredibly powerful. I can completely
control her body. What an incredible
turn-on! I have the capability to drive
the woman I love completely out of her mind.
She could always do it to and for me
but I could never do it to or for her.
Boy, I sure can now.
My orgasm was incredibly intense
because I knew I had given her and
while I was teasing her, I was teasing
myself too.

I now want to go back and re-read how
to give her multiple orgasms. She's never
done that before & I bet I can help her
do that too. Frankly, I want to achieve that
because I have a rather voracious sexual
appetite with the ability to come three
times in an hour. If I can get her turned
on rather than hurt and frustrated - hopeful

she'll want to make love so that I can come more than once **in** a session.

~~████████~~

She fell asleep afterward holding my hand. I can't remember that ever happening and you can't believe how good that felt to me.

NOW, — how have you changed my life.

① I can't tell for sure yet in all the sexual aspects but if you write me a note and tell me you're interested I'll write you again in 6 months ~~if you write me~~ if ~~back and tell~~ me you'd like to hear more. I'll tell you how we're doing in bed

② ~~As I say~~ I believe you've saved my marriage. I LOVE MY WIFE. She's bright, articulate, attractive, a wonderful mother for our 3 kids, and she's my best friend. We've always been able to talk about anything openly and honestly except for sex. Our marriage has been a beautiful cooperative partnership, except for sex. (She's a candidate for a Ph.D. and will receive it in the Spring of 192.) The kids and I have supported her through all of that.
A long time ago I realized I loved this woma

deeply and although our sex life was lousy — everything else was too good to give up. I tried to "live" with it. My male ego was hurt badly and I was increasingly tempted to seek out a "responsive bed partner" to fill that void. I was even thinking that cheating would help keep my marriage together. The saddest part is that if I had decided to cheat and found a good "faker" I might have eventually left my wife.

<u>What a stupid and dangerous game.</u>

From an: emotional standpoint
          getting caught standpoint
          <u>disease</u> standpoint ———> and family
hurting and losing my wife standpoint.
But I was feeling that desperate. I thought
it was the only way to keep my marriage together.
I was so emotionally hurt it was the only
way I saw I could fill the void.

<u>I DON'T NEED TO DO THAT ANYMORE.</u>

My mental state is wonderful this morning.

(3) I quit smoking this morning. I now want
to live a long life with my wife &
have every reason to live. I was
smoking and drinking too much. It was
clearly stifling my sex drive some — not
alot. Since we were down to having
sex three times a week (I was still
masturbating 7 times a week) it helped
some but it was also killing me. I now
know I will be able to get both out
of my life. (smoking & drinking)
I am happier than I have been in a long time.

Finally, perhaps I can do something for you. When you're on a talk show in the future I'd sure like to know. I'd love to call in and tell people the importance of your book. You are an incredible woman. I can only grieve for ——— my first 18 years of marriage based on my ignorance.

Use any of this letter that will help you promote the book. I'm going to sign my name to this letter because I want you to know every word is true — although I suspect you already know that it is. Please don't use my name, not because it would bother me but because it would hurt ~~bother~~ my wife.

I only wish the book could be given to every couple that applies for a marriage license. I don't know how much the divorce rate would be reduced but I believe it would reduce it some. Some percentage of couples get divorced because of sexual incompatibility and Betty and I could have ended up that way. YOU'VE CHANGED MY LIFE!

I sincerely hope that you get a chance to

write me, I feel like you're a friend.
If you are doing an appearance in Washington, D.C. area please let me know, I'd just like to thank you personally. There's a great deal more I'd like to say but I think this letter is longer than ~~your~~ book. Even if you don't get to read the letter, I feel better for having written it.

THANK YOU AND LET ME KNOW IF THERE IS ANYTHING I CAN DO FOR YOU.

If you do write please send it to my company address marked personal & confidential

thanks ⸺

PS. Please forgive the hand written, rambling nature of this letter I couldn't ask my secretary to type it!

Afterword

To all you men out there who are putting into action what you've just read, and are no longer practicing THE BIG BANG THEORY, but are, with much love, gently and tenderly pleasuring your women . . .

thank you . . .

And to all you women no longer faking it, but enjoying sex completely, with warm feelings and open hearts, who are with much love and passion pleasuring your men . . .

thank you . . .

because from all of you who are giving and receiving and making love, lots of that love is spilling over and touching all the rest of us, and because we're all connected, when you're more loving it touches me, and when I'm more loving it touches you.

We're all in this together, and love makes us know we're all one.